You Are a Boy

The Bible Tells Me So Press

You Are a Boy

A children's book produced by
The Bible Tells Me So Press

PUBLISHED BY
THE BIBLE TELLS ME SO CORPORATION
WWW.THEBIBLETELLSMESO.COM

First Printing October, 2019

You are
a
boy,

and you're
a delight.

God
carefully
formed

and made you just right.

Before you
were born,

God planned
when and how

He'd make you to be

the boy
you are now.

He made
no mistakes,
we hope you're aware,

because God made you
with caution
and care.

So know
when you're
big

and
know
when you're small,

God made you a boy,

there's
no doubt at all.

And know
every day,

we're filled
with such
joy

that you're
an awesome,

perfectly-made boy!

For it was You who formed
my inward parts;
You wove me together in my
mother's womb.
I will praise You, for I am awesomely
and wonderfully made;
Your works are wonderful,
And my soul knows it well.

Psalm 139:13-14

For more
books, videos, songs, and crafts,
visit us online at
TheBibleTellsMeSo.com

Standing on the Bible and growing!